CW01190143

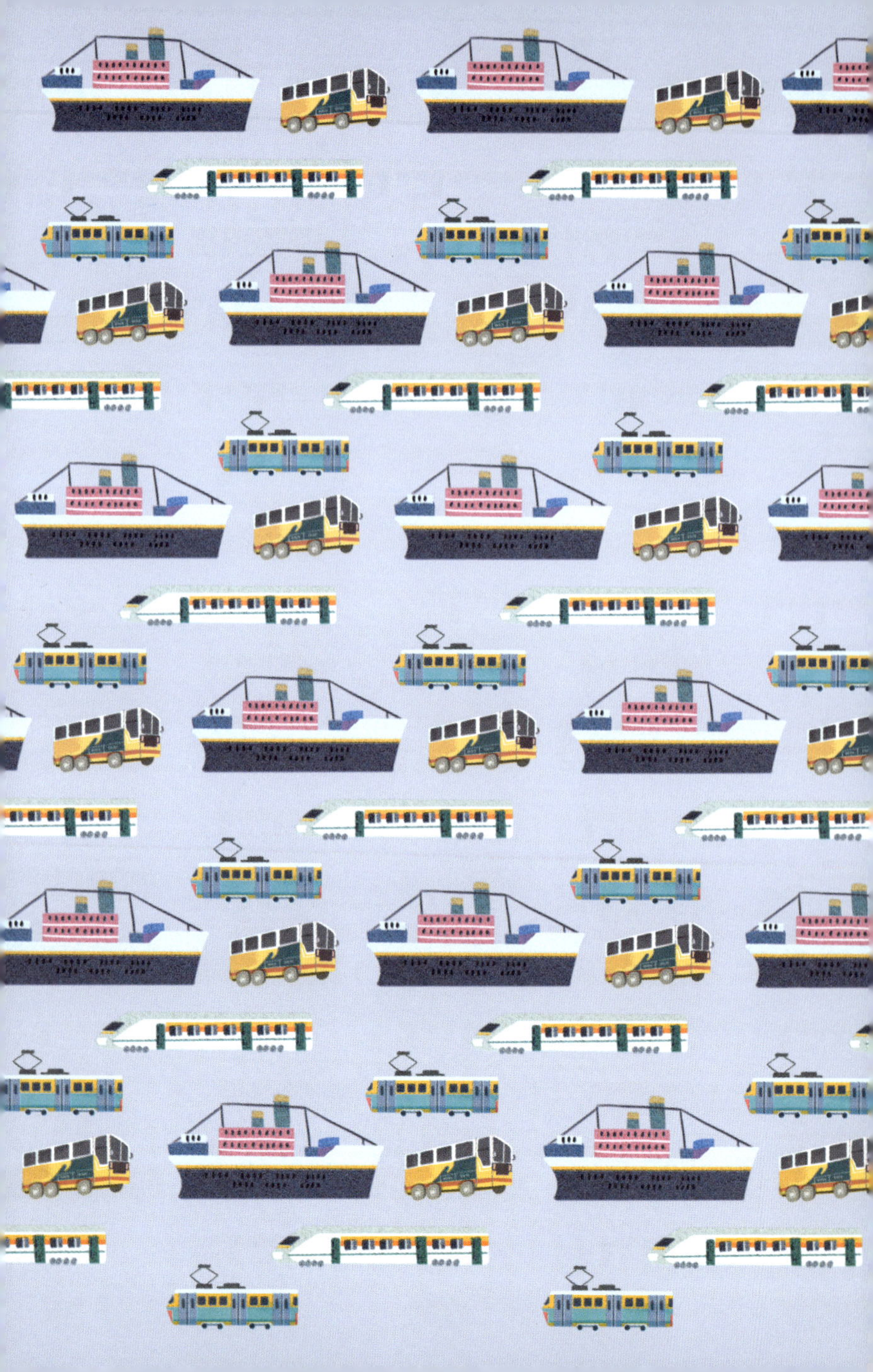

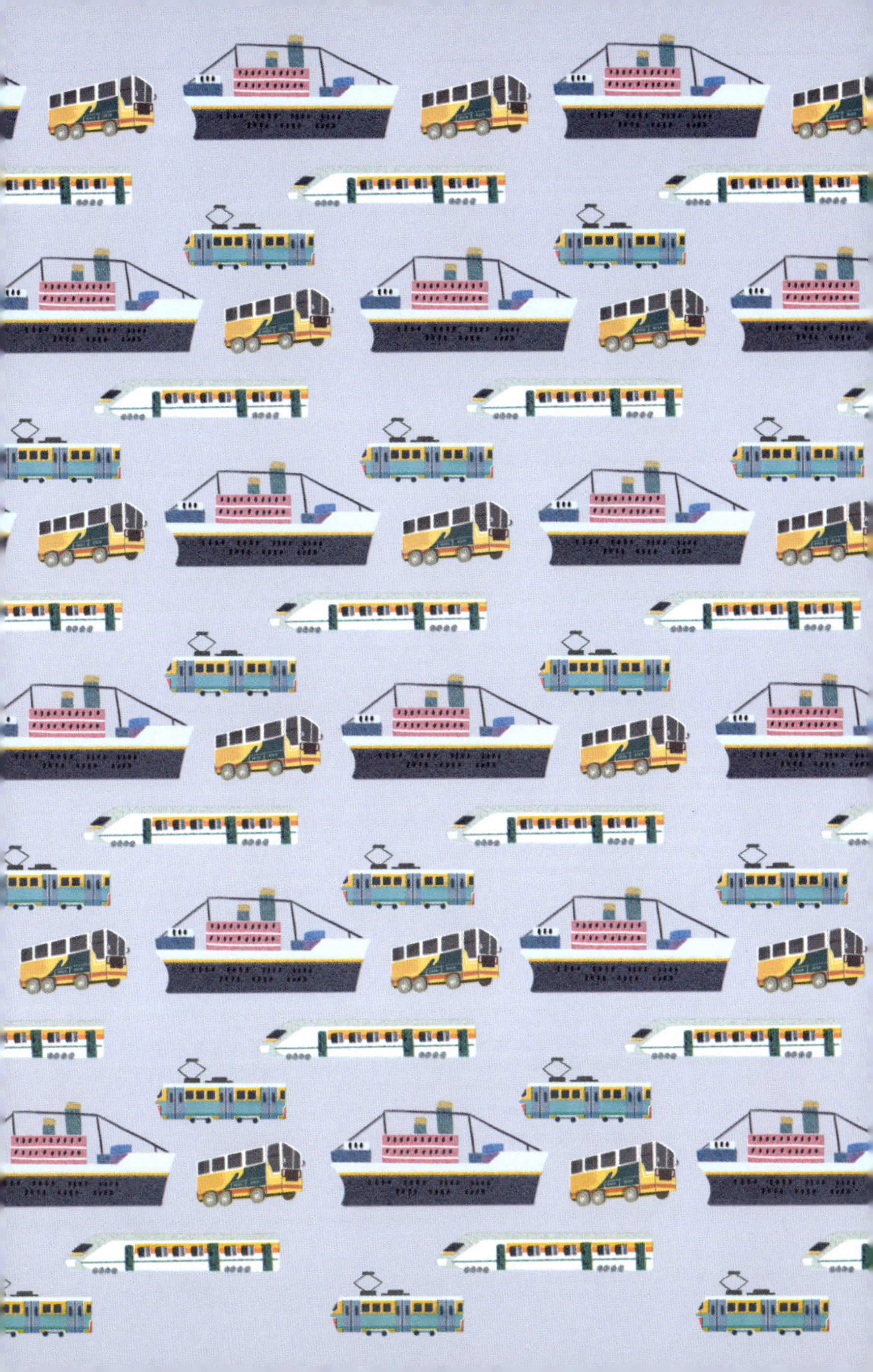

OXFORD
UNIVERSITY PRESS

Great Clarendon Street, Oxford, OX2 6DP,
United Kingdom

Oxford University Press is a department of the University of Oxford. It furthers the University's objective of excellence in research, scholarship, and education by publishing worldwide. Oxford is a registered trade mark of Oxford University Press in the UK and in certain other countries

Text © Oxford University Press 2023

The moral rights of the author have been asserted

First edition published in 2023

All rights reserved. No part of this publication may be reproduced, stored in a retrieval system, or transmitted, in any form or by any means, without the prior permission in writing of Oxford University Press, or as expressly permitted by law, by licence or under terms agreed with the appropriate reprographics rights organization. Enquiries concerning reproduction outside the scope of the above should be sent to the Rights Department, Oxford University Press, at the address above.

You must not circulate this work in any other form and you must impose this same condition on any acquirer

British Library Cataloguing in Publication Data

Data available

ISBN: 978-1-382-04339-7

10 9 8 7 6 5 4 3 2

The manufacturing process conforms to the environmental regulations of the country of origin.

Printed in China by Golden Cup

Acknowledgements

The publisher and author would like to thank the following for permission to use photographs and other copyright material:

Illustrated by Jeiting Chen and Kate McLelland.

Back Cover: ben bryant / Shutterstock. Photos: p30(t): Design Pics Inc / Alamy Stock Photo; p30(m): Catuncia / iStock / Getty Images; p30(b): Frank Günther / iStock / Getty Images Plus; p34, 46(a) : Sean Pavone / Shutterstock; p35: RZAF_Images / Alamy Stock Photo; p36: Hemis / Alamy Stock Photo; p37(t): Galyna Andrushko / Shutterstock; p37(b), 46(b): South America / Alamy Stock Photo; p38: Paulharding00 / Shutterstock; p39: Gary Cook / Alamy Stock Photo; p40: byvalet / Shutterstock; p41, 46(c): Sundry Photography / Shutterstock; p42(tl): ben bryant / Shutterstock; p42(tr): Leonid Andronov / Shutterstock; p42(b), 46(d): Karol Kozlowski / Shutterstock; p43: SankyPix / Shutterstock.

Every effort has been made to contact copyright holders of material reproduced in this book. Any omissions will be rectified in subsequent printings if notice is given to the publisher.

MIX
Paper | Supporting responsible forestry
FSC® C110497

Night Trip 9

Lots of Trips 29

OXFORD
UNIVERSITY PRESS

ai as in wait

ee as in sheep

igh as in night

oa as in road

was

her

A night trip on rails is fun.

STOP AND THINK

Think of things we might see.

NIGHT TRIP

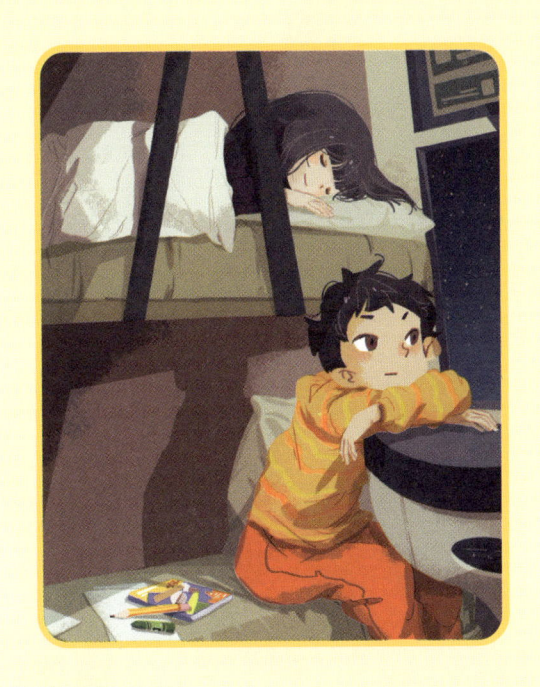

Written by Lucy Morgowr
Illustrated by Jieting Chen

Cheng Fan of ...

pets

dim sum

Ning Fan of ...

comics

fish and chips

8:30pm

We will travel to see Nan and Grandad tonight.

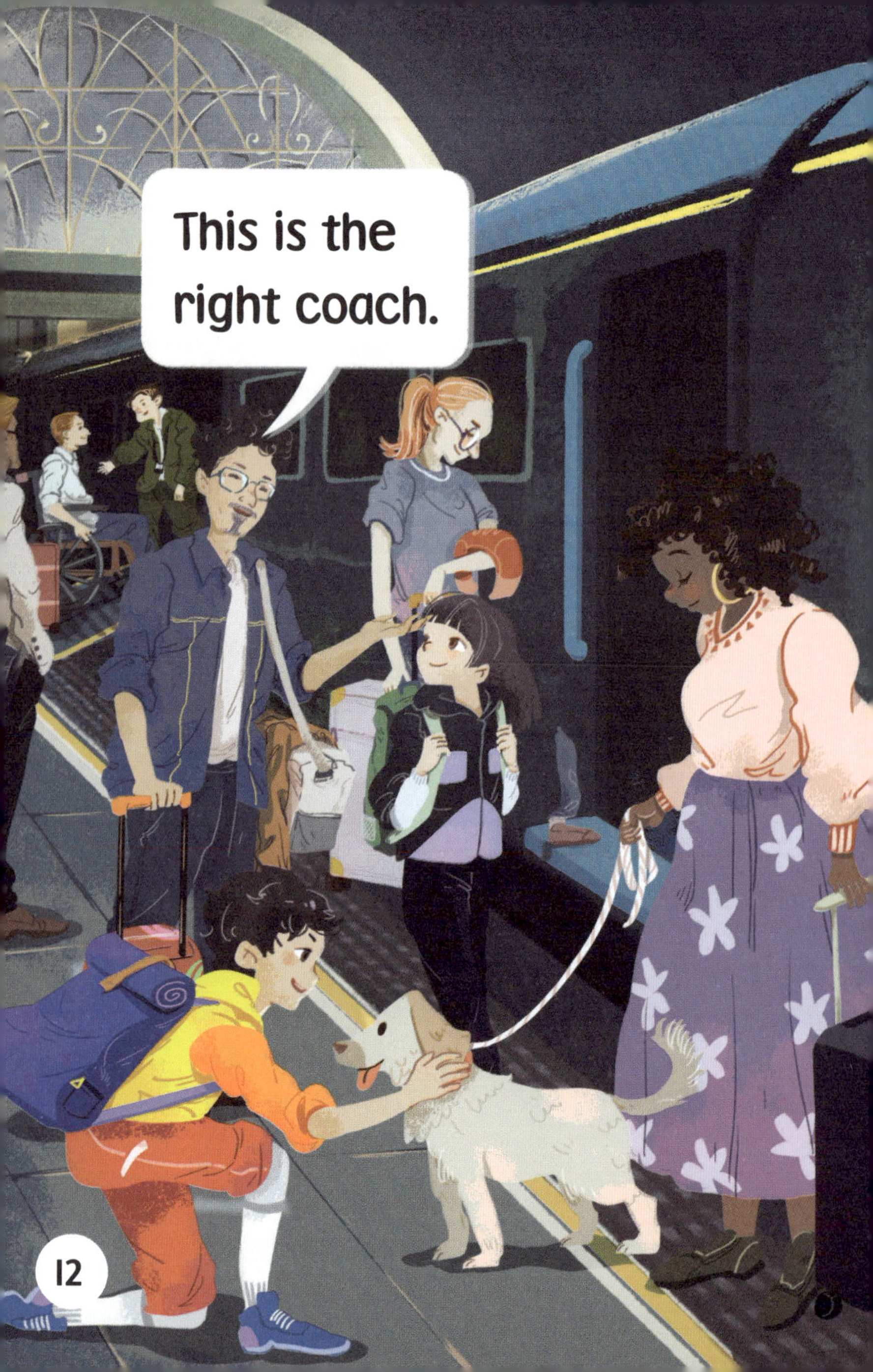
This is the right coach.

Dad puts his coat in his cabin.

We set off.

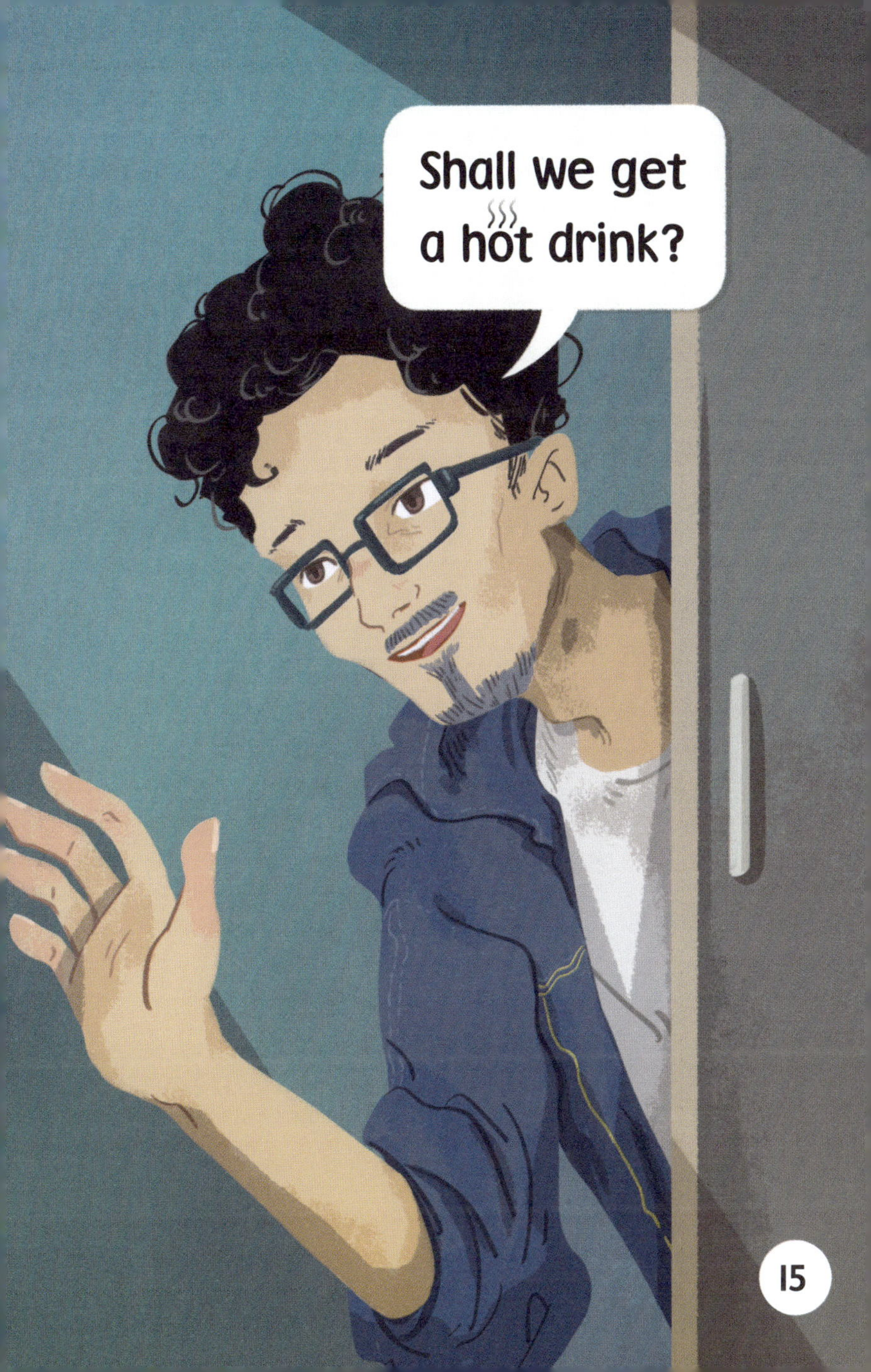
Shall we get a hot drink?

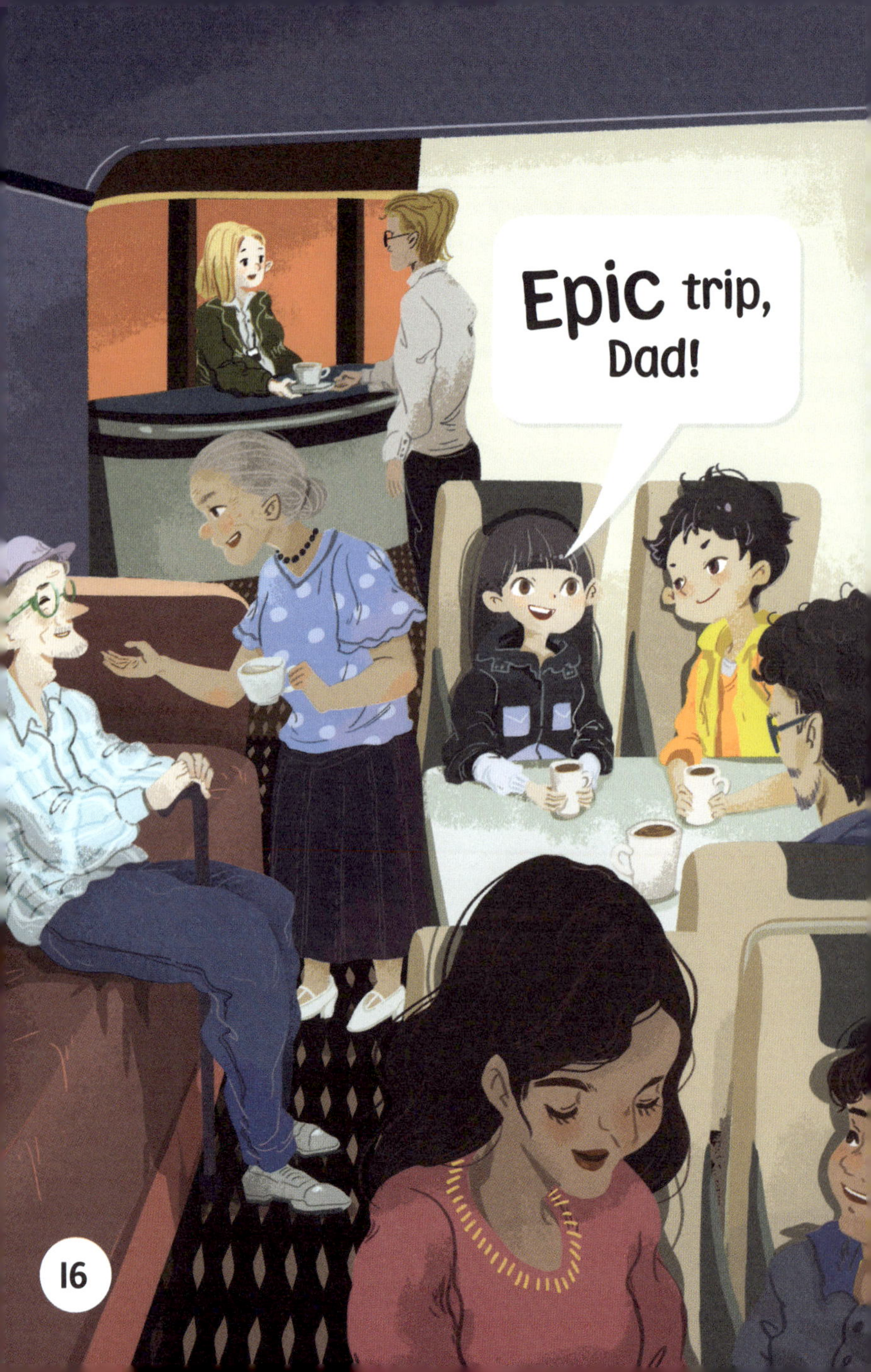
Epic trip, Dad!

Night!

I bet I will not rest!

Ning feels snug in her bed.

We might get fish and chips!

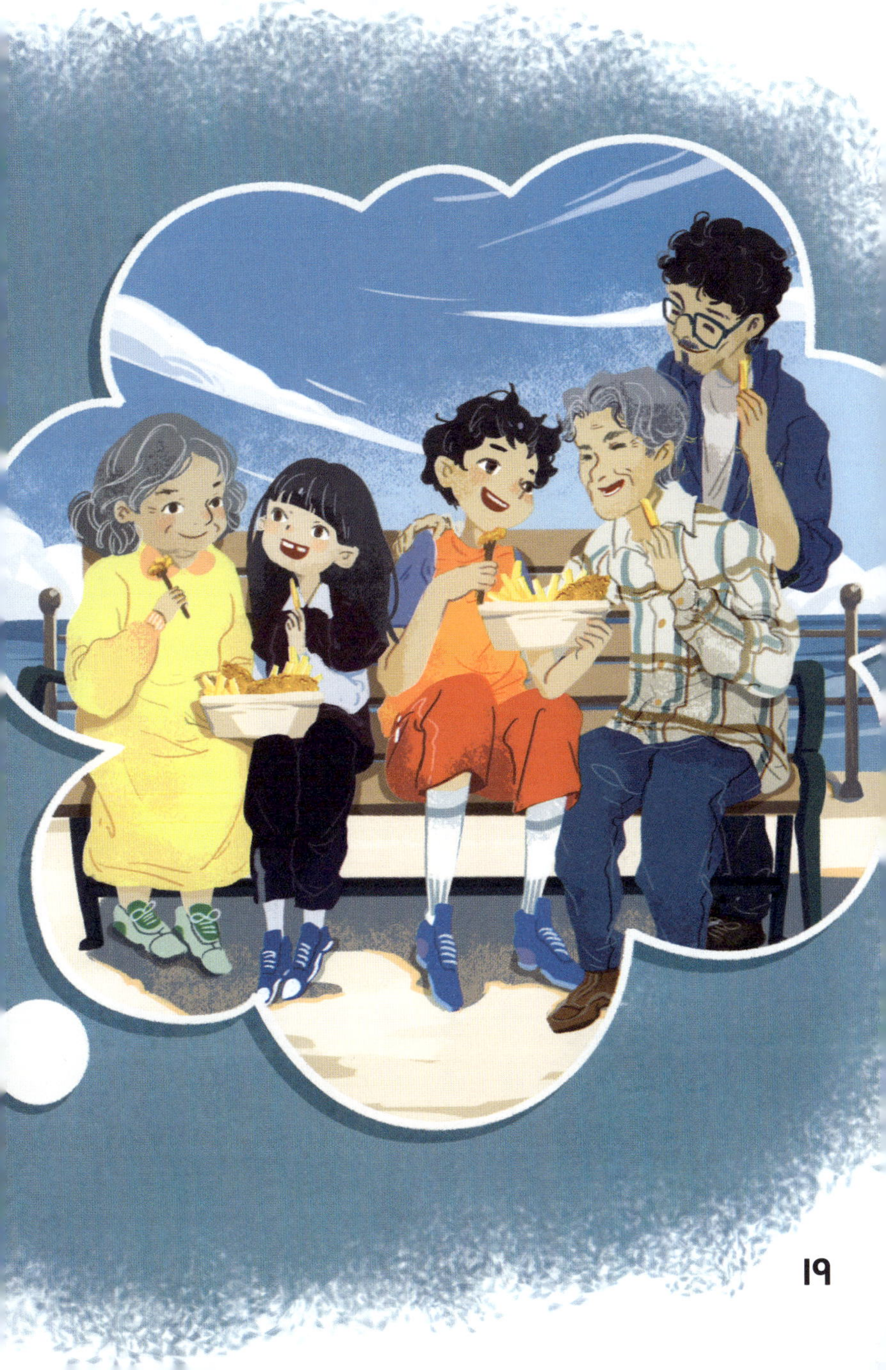

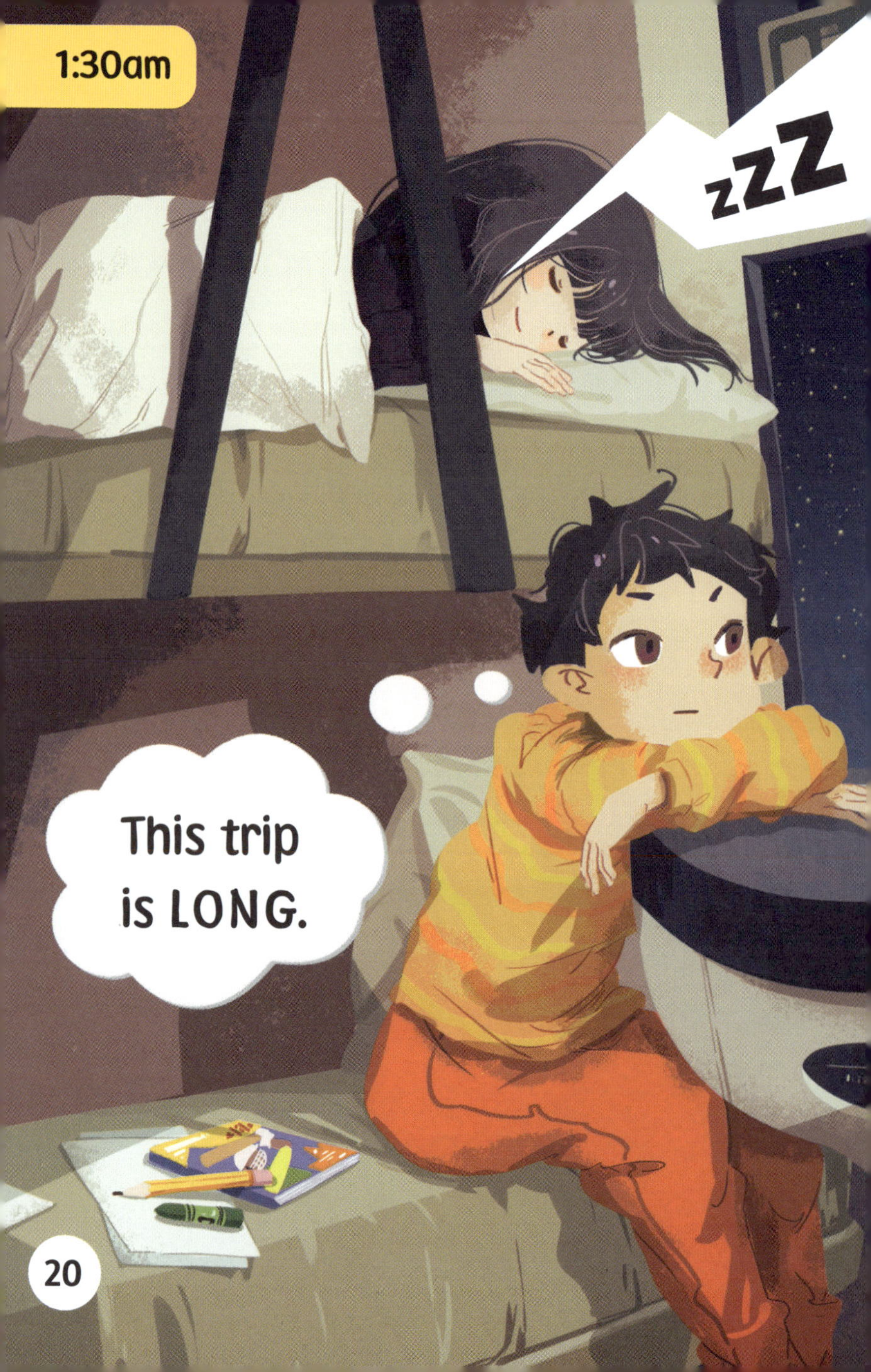
1:30am
zZZ
This trip is LONG.

Map of the rail trip

The End

5:15am

Ning gets up to see the boats.

6am

Ning packs her bag.
Dad sees the map.

It is fab, Cheng!

6:30am

We go into a forest, then a tunnel.

This is it!

We need to get off.

Was it a fun trip?

Yes! I did not go to bed!

Zzzz

27

Plan a fun epic trip.

STOP AND THINK

Will it be on a boat? Will it be on rails and the road?

LOTS OF TRIPS

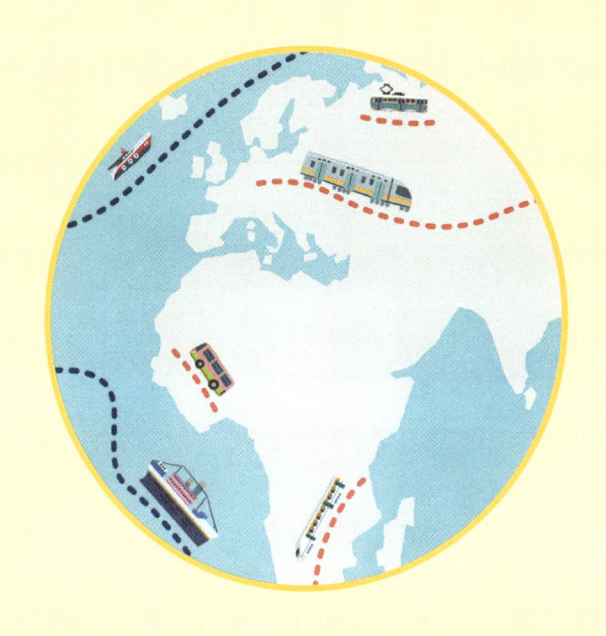

Written by Lucy Morgowr
Illustrated by Jieting Chen

We can go on **epic** trips.

on roads

on rails

on boats

Bob is a fan of travel.
He was on a trip
but got LOST!

Bob

He had a nap on a boat.

ZZZz

This was <u>not</u> the plan!

We can plan a long trip.

Get a map!

33

Rail

We can go across **JAPAN**.

We can travel in **KENYA**.

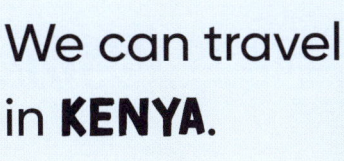

We might see zebras!

Kenya

We can go on rails to **DARWIN**!

Boat

Reed boats can go on **LONG** trips.

37

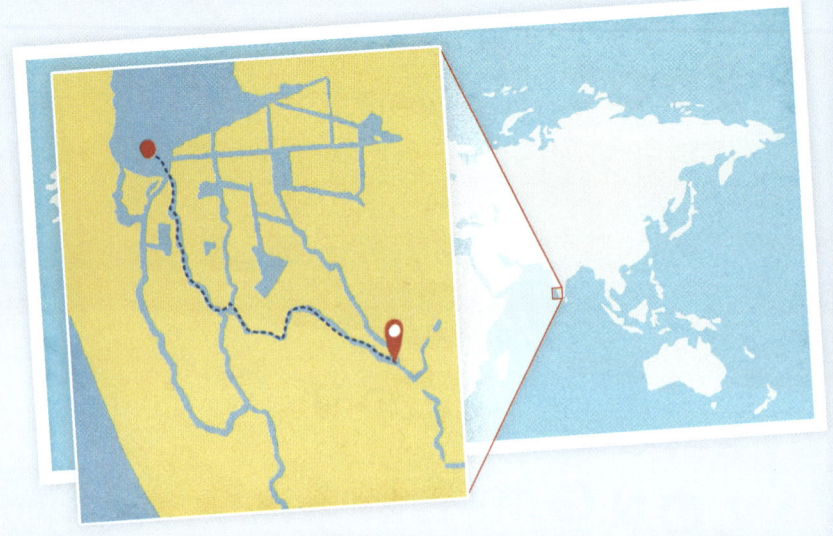

This boat **SAILS** past the trees.

He stands up in this boat.

Delta

This boat is in the Delta.

We can spend weeks on a **BIG** ship.

Road

A bus can go on long trips.

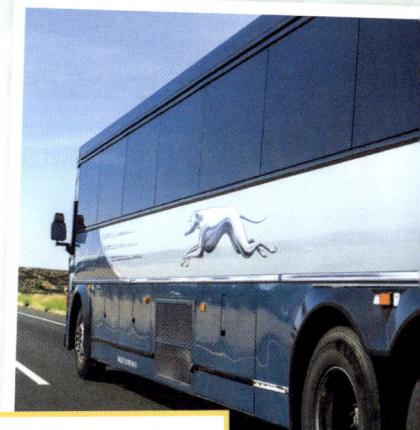

This bus travels to Canada.

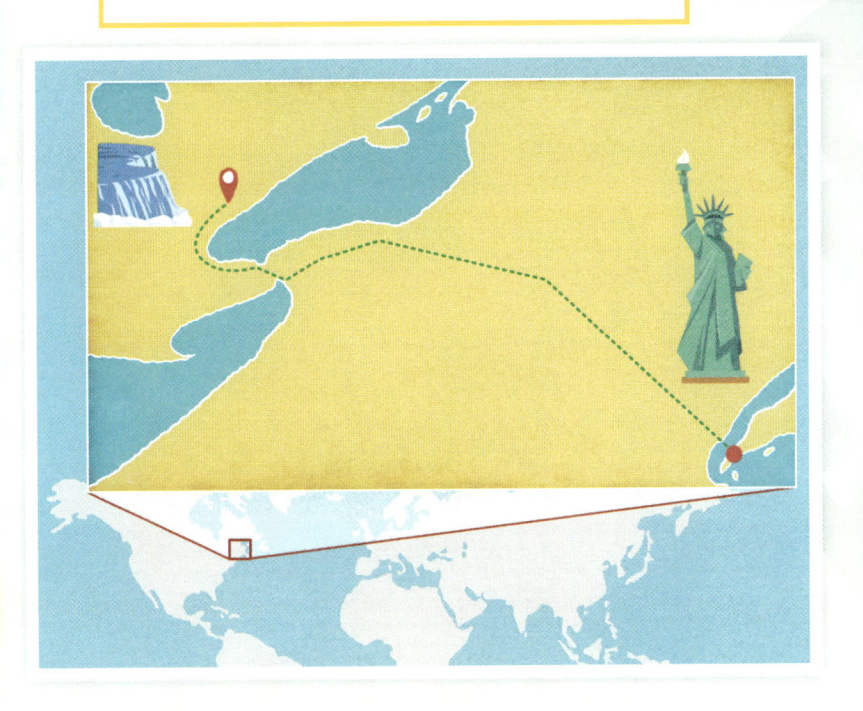

41

Trams can be **fun** to go on.

This tram is off to the sand.

Pick an **epic** trip!

Rail, boat, road?

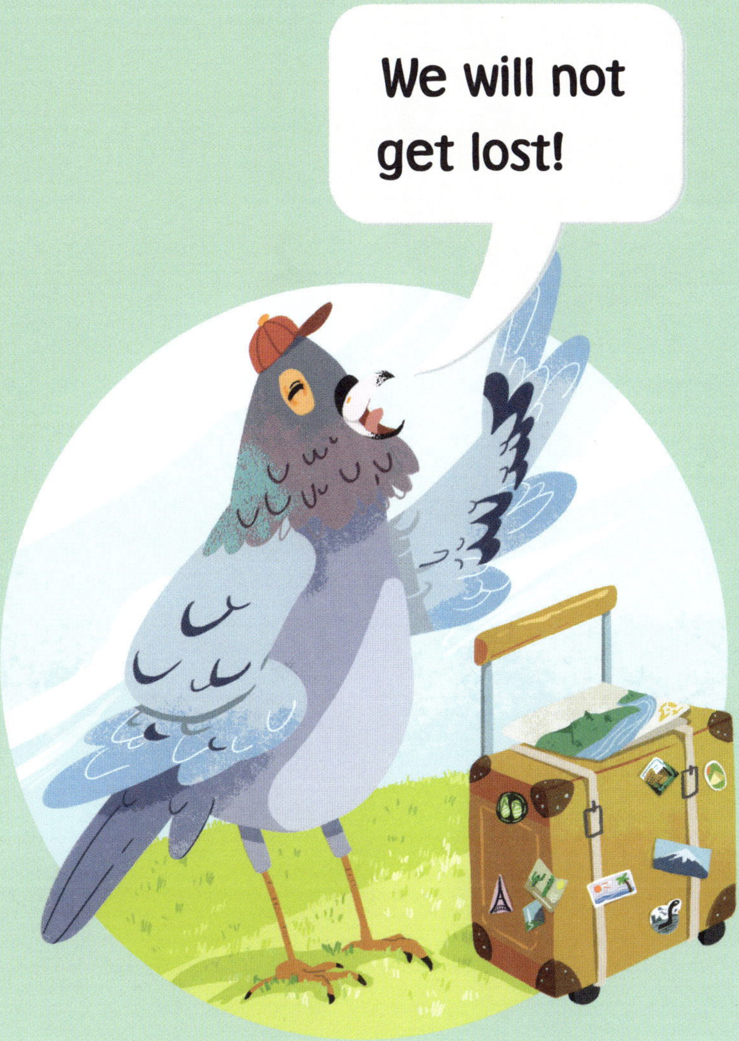
We will not get lost!

1

2

3

4

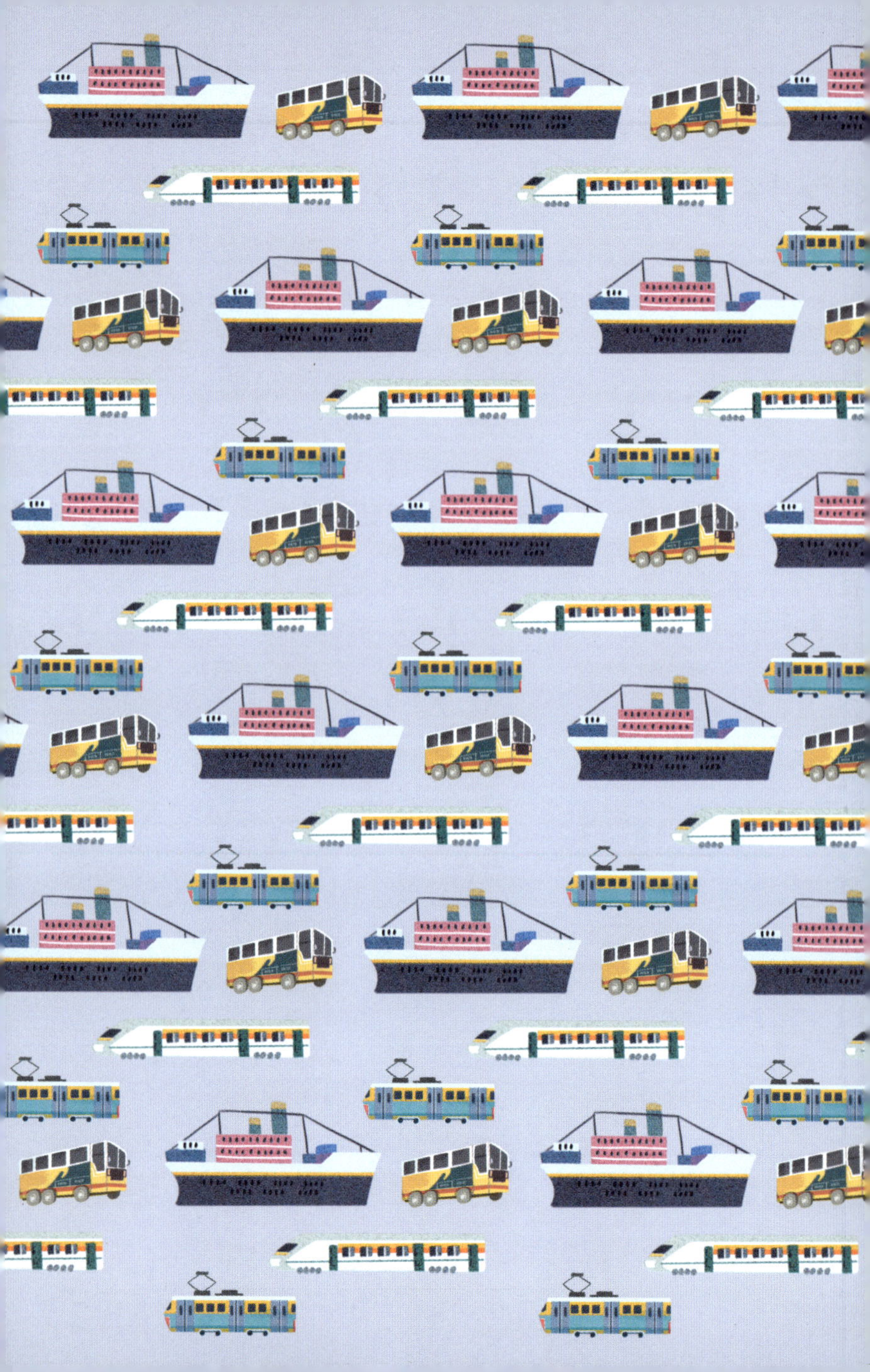